HIDDEN BY THE CLOUDS

SWEET & SOUR POETRY

By David Prestbury

First Edition
Published by David Prestbury 2008
Through Lulu.com
IBSN 978-0-95597777-2-5

All Poems
Drawings & Photo's are by the Author (David Prestbury)
Apart from the School Photo 'Laura Jo' on page 7
Photo of David Prestbury 'An Invitation' was taken by
My son Jaimie Lee Prestbury in Nairn,Scotland

Photo's 'For' & Dave in Spetze (Greece)
& Dave on the rocks in Ibiza (Spain) on page 7
Were taken by my ex-wife Carol Ann Prestbury

Photo's 'David Prestbury 2008 page 108
& 'The Moon' on page79 were both taken by
My brother Philip Prestbury

Front Cover Design
(The Clouds over Looe, in Cornwall, England)

& Back Cover Design
(Sand Pools in Nairn, Scotland)
Are also by the Author (David Prestbury)

The Illustration on Page19 'Loving Moments'
Was drawn by My Daughter Laura Joanne Prestbury

FOR

MY FANTASTIC FAMILY
& FRIENDS

LOVE YOU ALL

DAVE IN SPETZE (GREECE) 1985

AN INVITATION

TO ENTER
MY SOUL
MY INNER SELF

CONTENTS

DREAM

I SEARCHED HOPELESSLY FOR YOU
IN THE THICKNESS OF THE MIST & FOG

FALLING, SOMETIMES CRAWLING
HAD TO FIND YOU

SEEKING WITHOUT DIRECTION
ACHIEVING NOTHING ONLY DESPERATION

I CALLED OUT FOR YOU IN VAIN
ONLY A REVERBERATION OF YOUR NAME

I PURSUED YOU IN THE PARK
BUT YOU DISAPPEARED INTO THE DARK

I CHASED YOU THROUGH THE DISTANT TIME
AND LOST YOU IN THE MIST OF A DREAM

THE MOVING STAIRWAY

I WAS GOING UP
YOU WERE COMING DOWN

THE ESCALATOR STOPPED
THERE WAS NO ONE AROUND

NOT EVEN A SOUND
OUR EYES MET,

TRANSFIXED
TWO TOTAL STRANGERS

LOCKED BETWEEN
THE PAST AND FUTURE

ACHIEVING & CONCEIVING
IMAGINARY ORGASMS

NOW YOU ARE GOING UP
& I AM COMING DOWN

WITHOUT STOPPING,
WITHOUT TURNING

WITHOUT PAUSING,
WITHOUT EVEN A SOUND

OUR MISSION COMPLETED

A BRIEF MIDNIGHT BUS STORY

SITTING ON THE LATE BUS
THE TIME BEING MIDNIGHT
FEELING QUITE NONCHALANT

TIRED AND A LITTLE TIGHT
GLANCING AROUND I FELT A SENSE
OF UNEASINESS CREEP IN ON ME

FOR SITTING DIRECTLY OPPOSITE
WAS AN ATTRACTIVE YOUNG GIRL
STARING SEDUCTIVELY AT ME

I GLARED MAGNETICALLY
AT HER LONG DARK HAIR
& HYPNOTICALLY INTO HER COAL BLACK EYES

THEN DOWN TO HER RAVISHING
MINI-SKIRTED BARE THIGHS
WANDERING TO MYSELF -

IF ONLY? (COMMUNICATION BARRIER)
THAT THING INBETWEEN
YOU KNOW WHAT I MEAN

LOOKED OUT OF MY SIDE WINDOW
THINKING IT FATE IT WAS MY STOP
 - HOW SAD! NOW IT'S ALL TOO LATE

UP OUT OF MY SEAT & ON MY WAY
I TOOK ONE LAST LOOK
INTO HER SPARKLING EYES IN VANE

AMIDST THE HEAD SHAKING & SIGHS
I WALKED DEJECTEDLY INTO
THE LONELY NIGHT'S POURING RAIN

KNOWING & GROANING TO MYSELF
THAT I'LL PROBABLY NEVER EVER SEE
THAT BEAUTIFUL FACE AGAIN (AND I DIDN'T!)

BREATHTAKING

YOU TAKE MY BREATH AWAY
THE WAY YOU WALK
THE WAY YOU SWAY

YOU TAKE MY BREATH AWAY
THE WAY YOU TALK
THE THINGS YOU SAY

YOU TAKE MY BREATH AWAY
THE WAY YOU KISS
THE WAY YOU LAY

YOU TAKE MY BREATH AWAY
EACH AND EVERY DAY
AND I AM OVERWHELMED

BY YOUR LOVELINESS & SEXINESS
THAT LEAVES ME BOTH
HELPLESS & BREATHLESS

LIKE I SAY
YOU TAKE MY BREATH AWAY

LOVE ON THE ROCKS

SITTING BY THE SEA-SHORE
LISTENING TO THE SAVAGE SOUND OF WILD WAVES
AS THEY GO LASHING, CRASHING & RAGING AGAINST
THOSE SEA-WEED GREEN & GREY RAVAGED ROCKS

ADMIST THE SPITTING SPUME,
FIZZING FROTH & SEA-SPRAY
I OBSERVE THE SHRIEKING SHRILL OF SEA-GULLS
AS THEY SKY-DIVE, SWOOP, GLIDE

THEN SUDDENLY SOAR & TAKE FLIGHT
THROUGH THE CLUSTER
OF STORM CLOUDS
AND OUT OF SIGHT

THIS IS THE PLACE I LOVE & LONG TO BE
SITTING ON THE ROCKS
WITH YOU, MY LOVE
BEING SEDUCED BY THE SAVAGE SEA

WITNESSING THE SLEEPY SUNRISE
WHEN THERE'S NO ONE AROUND
LISTENING TO THE LAZY LAPPING SOUND
& WHISPERNG SAND WITH YOU HOLDING MY HAND

GIVING IT A GENTLE SQUEEZE
YOUR WINDSWEPT HAIR BLOWING
IN THE SALT-SEA BREEZE
STARING FAR OUT AT THE SILVERY SEA

AT THE EARLY MORNING FISHING BOATS
WATCHING THE FISHERMENS' CATCH
AS THEY DRAG & HOIST THEIR FISH FILLED NETS
UP & ONTO THEIR SALT SODDEN DECKS

SQUINTING AT A DISTANT
SAUNTERING SAILING SHIP
HANKERING OVER THE HORIZON
THEN DISAPPEARING INTO THE SUNSET

CATCHING A GLIMPSE
OF A WAVE WEAVING WINDSURFER ON DISPLAY
& A COUPLE OF SKINNY DIPPERS IN THE BAY
AS WE KISSED EACH OTHER PASSIONATELY

THIS IS THE PLACE I LOVE & LONG TO BE
WHEN ALL IS TRANQUIL & STILL
SITTING HERE WITH YOU, MY LOVE
GIVES ME SUCH A THRILL

AS WE WRITE OUR NAMES
IN THE SANDS OF TIME
I AM YOURS
AND YOU ARE MINE

SUMMER DREAMS

LET US SAIL
ON THE SILVER SEA

BETWIST THE SUN & SHADE
WHERE DREAMS ARE MADE

LET US SAIL
ON THE SALT SEA BREEZE

JUST YOU & I
AGAINST THE SKY BLUE SKY

SHARING SUMMER DREAMS

A VISUAL LOVE

A GENTLE SUMMERS' RAIN
FALLS SPLASHING, SLASHING

ACROSS YOUR SOFT
WARM SENSUAL FACE

SO PASSIONATELY
I TOUCHED & KISSED

YOUR WET FOREHEAD
YOU SMILED AT THE CARESS

NO WORDS WERE SPOKEN
NO WORDS WERE NEEDED

FOR OUR EYES HAD SPOKEN
BOTH SENSUALLY & SILENTLY

& WITH A LIGHT OF TENDERNESS
A VISUAL LOVE GROWS

YOU

YOU ARE AS REFRESHING
AS ICE COLD MILK
ON A HOT SUMMERS' DAY

YOU ARE AS INNOCENT
AS THE FRECKLES
AROUND A SMALL CHILD'S NOSE

YOU ARE AS PLEASANT
AS THE COMING OF THE SPRING
THE RUSTLE OF AUTUMN LEAVES

A GENTLE SUMMER'S BREEZE
A WINTER'S SNOWSCENE
BEFORE THE FREEZE

YOU ARE-
MY LOVE ALL THESE
THINGS TO ME

- I LOVE YOU

DAUGHTER LAURA JO (16)

11

AUTUMN EYES

I LOVE YOUR AUTUMN EYES
THE WAY YOU LOOK AT ME

YOUR SOFT WARM GENTLE SMILE
I LOVE YOU PASSIONATELY

I LOVE THE WAY YOU
LOVE OUR CHILDREN

THE WAY YOU LOVE ME
I LOVE YOU FOR BEING YOU

MY ANGEL
I LOVE YOU TENDERLY

TIME SCHEDULE

I MISSED THE BUS
   YOU MISSED THE TRAIN
       WE NEVER SAW
           EACH OTHER AGAIN......

THE MELANCHOLY
OF DEPARTURE

HOLDING BACK THE EMOTION
WHEN A LOVER SAYS GOODBYE

HOLDING BACK THE EMOTION
WHEN YOU SEE A LOVER CRY

HOLDING BACK THE EMOTION
WHEN THE TRAIN MOVES SLOWLY AWAY

LEAVING ME THE TIME AND
THE DISTANCE BETWEEN YOU

HOLDING BACK THE EMOTION
UNTIL AT NIGHT, WITHOUT THE LIGHT

A SAD AND LONELY TEAR
SHATTERS YOUR EMOTION BARRIER

AND YOU,
YOU CRY YOURSELF TO SLEEP

HELLRAISER

YOU PUT THE '**L**' INTO MY LIFE
YOU HORNY LITTLE SHE DEVIL YOU!

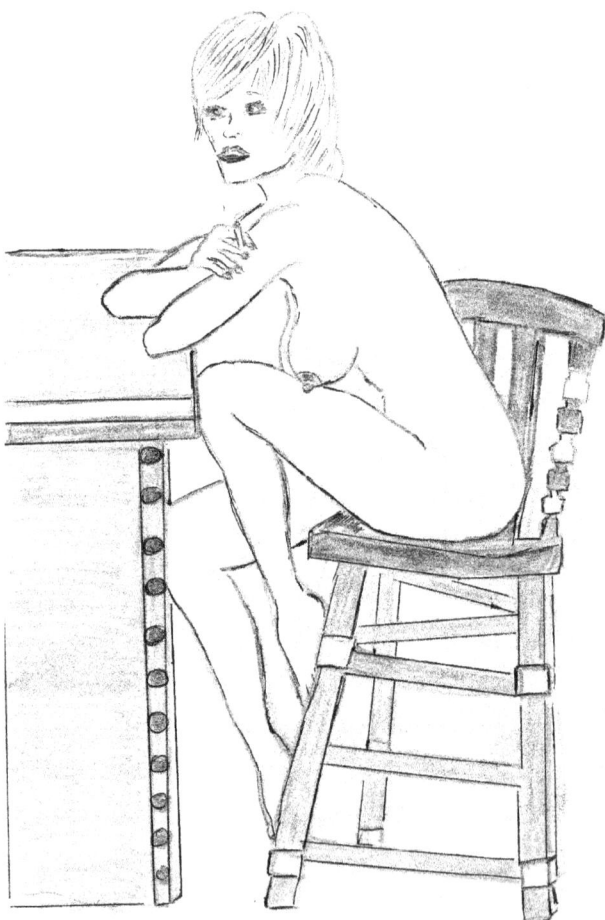

AN INTOXICATING LOVE AFFAIR

I SEE YOU
THROUGH A DRUNKEN-LIKE VISION
A BLURRED IMAGE OF BEAUTY
IS ALL I SEE

I HERE YOU
THROUGH A DRUNKEN-LIKE DRAWL
THE SLURRED SOUND
OF YOUR SWEET VOICE IS ALL I HEAR

I KISS YOU
ON YOUR COLD, WET SENSUAL MOUTH
THE FLAVOUR OF YOUR
PERNOD-LIKE BREATH IS ALL I TASTE

DISCO DOLLY BIRD

STATUESQUE,
WELL SCULPTURED
A SEXUAL DELIGHT

DIALOGUE
UNCULTURED,
OFTEN TRITE

PRETENTIOUS POSEUR
TRENDY & VAIN
NEVER A LOSER

BUT ALWAYS A PAIN

STATUETTE

YOU STAND
MOTIONLESS
NAKED

IVORY WHITE
PUBIC HAIRLESS
STARING EXPRESSIONLESS

INTO NOTHINGNESS

SHINING STAR

YOU CATCH THE SUN
AS I STAND IN YOUR SHADOW

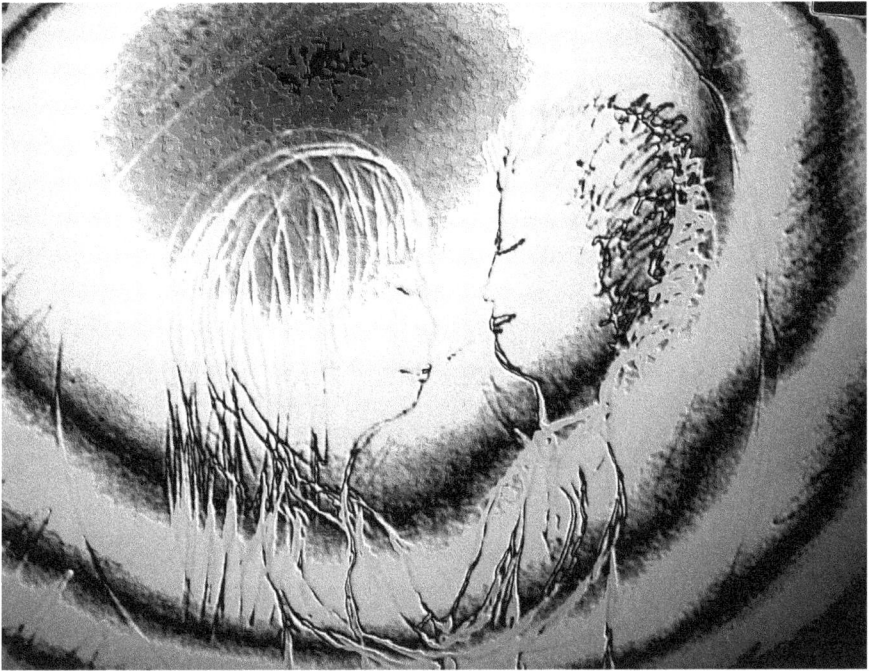

LOVING MOMENTS

ONCE OUR LOVE WAS BLIND
NOW I LOVE YOU WITH EYES OPEN WIDE

I LOVE YOU TODAY
I WILL LOVE YOU MORE TOMORROW

YOU & I ARE ONE
LIFE AS JUST BEGUN

ON COLD WET
MANCHESTER MORNINGS

ON COLD WET MANCHESTER MORNINGS
I WALK HAND IN HAND WITH YOU
KISSING, LAUGHING, TALKING

STROLLING THROUGH THE ROARING RAIN
AS IT CAME SHEETING DOWN
DRENCHING THE SODDEN STREETS OF OUR TOWN

THE SOGGY SOLES OF OUR SHOES
SQUELCHED AS WE TRUDGED THROUGH
THOSE OIL RAINBOW PUDDLES

WE SHELTERED
IN A CLOSED SHOP DOORWAY
ALONG THE WAY,

DRIPPING, SHIVERING, DITHERING
SOAKED TO THE SKIN
WE HUDDLED, CUDDLED & CARESSED EACH OTHER

I KISSED YOUR WET LIPS, YOU SMILED
AS I STARED INTO YOUR MISTY EYES
FULL OF LOVE, LUST & SURPRISE

WE WALKED ON EYE'S DOWN
MARVELING AT THE MOSAIC OF WHITE
CHEWING GUM STAINS

THAT DECORATED THE CITY PAVEMENTS
LEADING FROM VICTORIA TRAIN STATION
(WRIGLEY'S HAVE A LOT TO ANSWER FOR!)

UP TOWARDS SHUDEHILL
ONTO, MARKET STREET PICCADILLY,
WE SOLDIERED THROUGH

THE WIND & THE RAIN
TO OUR DESTINATION – OUR NEXT STOP
STARBUCK'S COFFEE SHOP,

AFTER AN EXPRESSO & CAPPUNCHINO
& TWO CHOCOLATE CHIP MUFFINS
& PLENTY OF TALKING OF SWEET NOTHINGS

WE VENTURED OUT AS THE RAIN FADED WAY
WE KISSED EACH OTHER GOODBYE
& WENT 'LOVES SWEET DREAMILY' ON OUR WAY

MY OTHER HALF

I WALK WITH YOU
I TALK WITH YOU

I EAT WITH YOU
I DRINK WITH YOU

LAUGH WITH YOU
CRY WITH YOU

GO TO BED WITH YOU
MAKE LOVE TO YOU

YOU ARE MY OTHER HALF
I LOVE YOU

WHO IS SHE?

WHO IS SHE?
WHO INSPIRES MY LIFE
WITHIN MY LIFE

WHO BEARS MY CHILDREN
WHO OFFERS HER INFINITE BEAUTY
WHO SMILES, SOMETIMES WEEPS

WHO LOVES, LIES BESIDE ME
WHO LIVES IN MY DREAMS
LIVES IN MY MIND

I LOVE HER IN FANTASY
I LOVE HER IN REALITY
MY WIFE

ALWAYS & FOREVER

I WILL LOVE YOU NOW MY LOVE
AS I HAVE LOVED YOU BEFORE

AND I WILL GO ON LOVING YOU MY LOVE
UNTIL I CAN LOVE NO MORE

EVER GET THAT FEELING?

EVER GET THAT FEELING
YOU CAN'T FORGET

LIKE YOUR BABY'S FIRST SMILE
& TAKE IT'S FIRST STEPS

YOUR CHILD'S ACHIEVEMENTS -
TOP MARKS IN EXAMS & TESTS

WHEN YOUR SON SCORES THE WINNING GOAL
AS THE BALL BURSTS THE BACK OF THE NET

WHEN YOU PASS
THAT NERVE WRACKING DRIVING TEST

WHEN THE LETTER SAY'S YOU'VE GOT THE JOB
OR PROMOTION 'COS YOU'RE SIMPLY THE BEST

WHEN YOUR LOVER WHISPERS I LOVE YOU
THAT FEELING YOU JUST CAN'T FORGET

MARRIAGE BLISS

SUNDAY MORNING

"LET'S MAKE LOVE, DEAR BRIDE,"
"I CAN'T! - THE CHILDREN
ARE PLAYING OUTSIDE,"

"COME ON LOVE, LET'S HAVE A NIBBLE,"
"OOOH! DO STOP THAT ERNEST,
YOU'RE MAKIN' ME GIGGLE,"

"AW! COME ON SUE, LET'S HAVE A SCREW,"
"SORRY LOVE I'VE ALL MY IRONING TO DO."
I SIGH! - IS THERE ANY USE BEING MARRIED TO YOU?

SUNDAY MIDDAY

"COME ON ERNEST, GIVE ME A KISS,"
"AW! COME ON SUE,
I'M GOING OUT ON THE P*SS,"

"ERNEST, DEAREST ERNEST,
OH! GIVE ME A LURRVE!!"
"GOOD HEAVENS ABOVE WOMAN! –

I'LL BE LATE FOR THE PUB'"
I SIGH! –
IS THERE ANY USE BEING MARRIED TO YOU?

SUNDAY EVENING

"ERNEST WAKE UP,
YOU DRUNKEN LOUT! -
YOU'RE SUPPOSED TO BE TAKING ME OUT,"

"OOH! DO STOP THAT SHAKIN' –
MI 'ED'S BLOODY ACHIN',
WHAT TIME IS IT SUE?"

"IT'S SEVEN THIRTY TWO & GERRIN' LATE
AND THE SITTER'S
COMING AT EIGHT,"

AT THE LOCAL (LATER THAT EVENING)

AFTER SIXTEEN PINTS & A BRANDY
SAY'S ERNEST - "HIC! –
I'M FEELIN' QUITE RANDY,"

"OOOH!" SAYS SUE,
WITH A SLIGHT GROAN -
"JUST WAIT 'TIL WE GERR HOME!"

LATER STILL THAT EVENING

BACK HOME & IT'S A RACE TO THE LOO
STAGGERS ERNEST UPSTAIRS TRAILING SUE
THEN ALL OF A SUDDEN BEFORE HIS VERY EYES

STANDS SUE ALL NAKED - RIGHT UP TO HER THIGHS
HE STRIPS HIMSELF OFF, OBLIGINGLY
GROANS SUE "TAKE ME! ERNEST - RAVISH ME!"

"I'M D D D DOING MI BEST –
OUCH! IT'S C C CAUGHT IN MI VEST
HELP ME SUE - I'M IN A BIT OF A STEW,"

SHE TEARS OFF HIS VEST
WITH SUCH PASSION AND ZEST
THEN IT'S OFF TO THE BEDROOM

LIKE TARZAN AND JANE
WHERE THEY EVENTUALLY HAVE IT –
AGAIN & AGAIN & AGAIN & AGAIN......

ARE THESE THINGS SENT TO TRY US?

HOW STRICT SHOULD WE BE WITH OUR CHILDREN?
THOSE DARLING LITTLE CREATURES OF OURS
WE TEACH THEM TO READ,
WE TEACH THEM TO WRITE

WE TEACH THEM TO CARE & TO SHARE,
NOT TO FUSS & FIGHT, SHOUT OR SWEAR
SHOW THEM POLITENESS, KINDNESS
GOOD MANNERS LIKE -

MAY I, THANK YOU AND PLEASE
TRY OUR BEST TO COPE –
WITH THEIR OVERBEARING
DEMANDS AND PLEADS -

OF "CAN I HAVE THIS MUM?" –
"CAN I HAVE THAT MUM?"
"WANT THIS! - WANT THAT!" –

"NEED THIS! - NEED THAT!"
"CAN YOU DO THIS DAD?" –
"CAN YOU DO THAT DAD?"
UNTIL THEY EVENTUALLY MAKE US

SCREAM, BAWL AND SHOUT -
"NO! STOP! DON'T! CAN'T!
MUSTN'T! SHOULN'T! GO! OFF! OUT!"
ARE WE LIMITING THEIR IMAGINATIONS

ARE WE ANTAGONISING THEIR FRUSTRATIONS
ARE WE BORING THEM, IGNORING THEM
WHEN WE SHOULD BE ENCOURAGING
AND ADORING THEM

ARE WE MISGUIDING THEM –
OVERRIDING THEM
ARE WE THE HYPOCRITS -
WHO PREACH WHAT'S RIGHT
AND WHAT'S WRONG

YOU SEE –
WE TELL THEM WHAT'S RIGHT
THEN DON'T DO OURSELVES WHAT'S RIGHT
BY DOING WHAT WE SAID WHAT'S WRONG

YES! THE ART OF PARENTCRAFT
IS SO BLOODY CONFUSING
THAT'S WHY MUMS HAVE DIZZY SPELLS
AND DADS GO OUT BOOZING.

"NO! YOU CAN'T HAVE MY COCONUT!"

FLIGHT TO MENORCA (99)

MY LITTLE 4 YEAR OLD SON 'JAIMIE LEE'
PANICKED WHEN OUR PLANE

FLEW SO HIGH
ABOVE THE CLOUDS

"OOOOH! DADDY! –
I 'FINK WE'RE IN HEAVEN!"HE WHISPERED

WITH A HINT OF FEAR
IN HIS LITTLE EYE

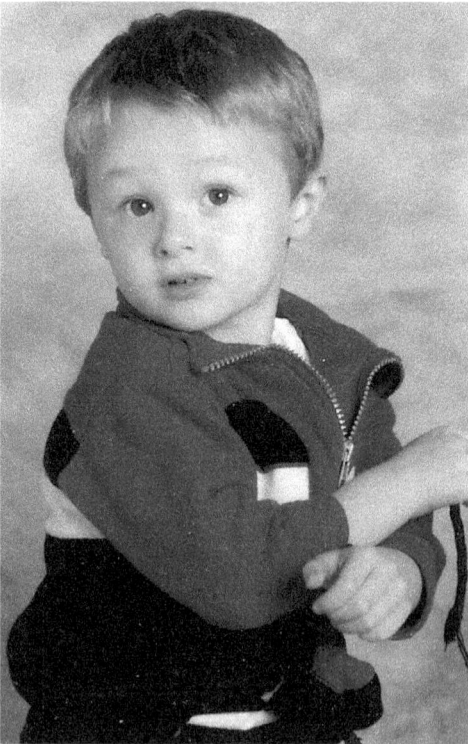

SON JAIMIE LEE

INACTION MAN

SON NICKY

"DDDDDAD!!
"FINK MY
'ACTION MAN'
IS SILLY"

"HOW DO YAH
MEAN SON?"

"WELL
HE CAN'T BE A
'MAN OF ACTION'

- COS' HE HASN'T
GOT A WILLY???"

LIFESPAN

"AWW!!! DDDAD!
DON'T YOU REALIZE?
BY MAKIN' ME GO TO BED
THIS EARLY
YOU'LL BE SHORTENIN' MY LIFE!"

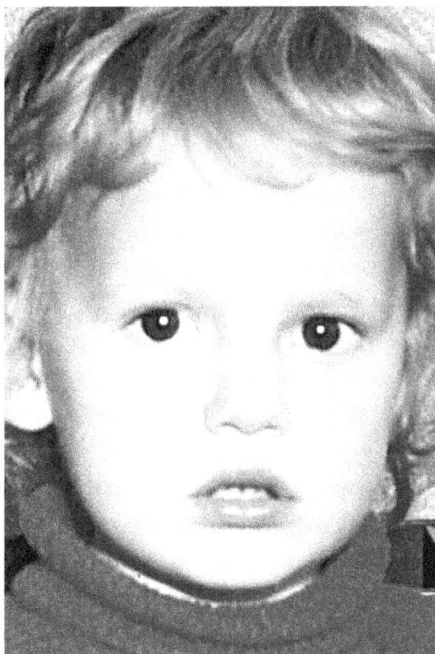

SON DAMIAN

29

PORTRAIT

YELLOW STRAW HAIR
VIOLET EYES WIDE
PURPLE LIPS THIN
PALE PINK SKIN

BLUE TEARS DRIPPING
DOWN HER CHIN
WITH SCARLET RED
ROSY CHEEKS

THIS IS A LITTLE LAD'S
IMPRESSIONISTIC
INTERPRETATION OF HIS MUM
(HE PAINTS HIS DAD IN BLACK & WHITE?)

TREADING ON EGGSHELLS

TAKE NO NOTICE - IT'S HER HORMONES
IGNORE HER -IT'S P.M.T.
TREAD CAREFULLY IT'S HER AGE
HEAVENS ABOVE SHE'S HAD IT ROUGH
SHE'S ON THE CHANGE,
SHE'S HAD IT ALL TAKEN AWAY

SO JUST BE CAREFUL
HOW YOU SAY THINGS
WHEN SHE SHOUTS & SCREAMS
'COS SHE'LL BITE YER BL**DIN' 'ED OFF
TELL YOU TO P*SS OFF & SHOUT OTHER
NASTY OBSCENE THINGS *#@#*!'#@#!

DUSTBIN DAD

AFTER US KIDS HAD FINISHED OUR TEA
DAD WOULD SEARCH FOR THAT LEFTOVER PEA
FISH FINGERS & PASTA, POTATOES & GREENS
PIES & PUDDS, EVEN BAKED BEANS

ANYTHING LEFTOVER - LIKE ICE-CREAM & JELLY
WOULD FIND ITSELF IN OUR DAD'S BELLY
HE'D MOP UP OUR DRINKS - OUR 'AFTERS' AS WELL
IT'S NO WONDER HIS TUMMY STARTED TO SWELL

IT GREW BIGGER & BIGGER
& MADE US KIDS SNIGGER
LIKE A ONE MAN EFFLUENT PLANT -
THE SIZE OF AN ELEPHANT

& WHEN HE LET OFF HIS GAS
FROM HIS MASSIVE BIG - BUM!
HE NEARLY BLEW
US KIDS TO KINGDOM COME!

A GREEDY OL' PIG-O-SAURUS
ONE HUNGRY HIPPOPOTAMUS
WHO COULD EAT FOR THE LOT-OF-US
IS OUR DUSTBIN DAD

PARP !!!

A WEIGHT OFF MY MIND

OH! I WISH I COULD LOSE WEIGHT
I REALLY WISH I COULD -
ROAST BEEF WITHOUT TH' YORKSHIRE PUD
CAN YOU IMAGINE WITH TWO VEG & ONLY ONE SPUD!

JUST A LITTLE BIT OFF MI BUM
& PLENTY OFF MI TUM
A WAIST LIKE A FLAMENCO DANCER
A BUM LIKE A BALLET DANCER

IF ONLY I COULD?
NO MORE FRY- UP'S FOR BREKKY
FULL SKIMMED MILK & NO SUGAR
FOR THIS SAD & FAT OL' BUGGER

OH! I WISH I COULD LOSE WEIGHT
I REALLY WISH I COULD
JOIN A SLIMMING CLUB
INSTEAD OF GOIN' TO TH' PUB

EXERCISE AT THE GYM
– GO FOR A JOG
OR TAKE A LAXATIVE
AND CAMP ON TH' BOG

NO MORE MINCE PIES
FOR OL' THUNDER THIGHS
NO CAKES OR CHOCCY BIC'S
NO RED MEAT & 'TATER PIES

WITH GREASY CHIPS
OH! TO BE NICE, NIMBLE & LIGHT
NO FLAB OR CELLULITE
NOT OBESE – NO WEIGH GAIN

JUST TO HAVE A TRIM WAISTLINE ONCE AGAIN
COUNTIN' TH' CALS – SWEATIN' ON TH' SCALES
IS THERE ANY HOPE FOR US BEACHED WHALES?
TRY LIPOSUCTION, A TUMMY TUCK

OR EVEN TH' FAT PILL
AND YOU CAN HAVE YOUR POUND O' FLESH
IF YOU JUST GIVE ME TH' WILL
TO LOSE THAT UNWANTED KILO

TO SLIP INTO MI 'OL MINI & HOT PANTS
I WORE IN MI PRIME
INSTEAD OF TH' MARQUEE TENTS
I WEAR ALL TH' TIME

OH! I WISH I COULD LOSE WEIGHT
I REALLY WISH I COULD
JUST GIVE ME THE WILL POWER – OH! LORD!
PLEASE LORD HAVE MERCY ON THIS FAT OL' SOD

LIFE'S A LOTTERY

IF ONLY MY CHILDREN WERE BORN
ON THE 'WINNING' DAYS

AND MY HOUSE NUMBER – THE BONUS BALL
IF ONLY LADY LUCK WOULD SHINE DOWN ON ME
(JUST FOR A WEE MILLION OR THREE)

OH! JUST TO HAVE IT ALL
- WOULDN'T LIFE BE AN ABSOLUTE BALL

FACTORY FODDER

LIFE'S ALL BUT
BELLS, BUZZERS,
SIRENS & HOOTERS

I ASK MYSELF
ISN'T LIFE
SO BLOODY ALARMING!

BRING BACK THE TEA LADIES

WELL, VENDING MACHINE
I'LL GET YOU NEXT TIME
YOU ROBBING SWINE
YOU, WITH YOUR CLEVER,
CLUMSY, FUMBLING
AUTOMATON HANDS

HAVE DONE IT AGAIN! –
UPENDING MY TEA
DELIBERATELY
DISOBEYING & IGNORING
MY FINGERTIPPED
COMMANDS

TEN PEE DOWN
THE BLOODY CHUTE
BUT YOU
COULDN'T
GIVE A HOOT
YOU ROBBING,

RIP OFF ROBOT
OF AN OVERSIZED
TIN CAN
I'LL KICK
YOUR ARSE,
I'LL SHAKE YOU -

I'VE A GOOD MIND
TO THROW YOU
TO THE GROUND
BUT YOU'D
JUST LIE THERE,
SO SMUG

HOLDING ON
TO MY TEN PEE
ALMOST
LAUGHING AT ME
BUT, I'LL GET YOU NEXT
TIME YOU SWINE,
I'LL GET YOU NEXT TIME (& I DID)

MESSAGE IN A 'THROTTLE'

INSIDE OF MY LUNCHBOX
A NOTE I DOTH FIND
A LINE OF POETRY
FROM MY WONDERFUL WIFE I WONDER?

A SORT OF 'SORRY MY LOVE'
OF THE PEACE OFFERING KIND
I REMOVED THE LID
WITH A SIGH! & PONDER

OH! WHAT MORE
CAN A MAN WANT OUT OF LIFE?
AFTER SUCH CRUEL WORDS
THE NIGHT BEFORE

TO DESERVE SUCH FLATTERY
FROM HIS LOVING WIFE
WHO WOULD THINK
T'WAS FAMILY AT WAR?

I EXTRACTED THE NOTE
FROM MY BOX THAT COMPRISED
OF FOUR CHEESE COBS & A CUSTARD
ALAS! IT READ TO MY GREAT SURPRISE –

TO HIS ROYAL HIGHNESS –
I HOPE THESE CHOKE YOU,
YOU B******
(RHYMES WITH CUSTARD)......

THE NIGHT IS YOUNG

THE NIGHT IS YOUNG
YET THE HOURS ARE OLD

MY LOVE GROWS WARM
WHILE YOUR LOVE GROWS COLD

SHOCK REACTION

YOUR ICE COLD WORDS
LEAVE ME SHIVERING, SHAKING

YOU ARE BITTER
I AM HURT

SPEECHLESS
FROZEN

ICICLE TEARS DEPICT SAD PATTERNS
UPON MY FROSTED FACE

I AM NUMBED, STUNNED
UPSET, MOVED

BY YOUR ICE COLD WORDS
YOUR ICE COLD EYES

THAT FREEZE MY SENSES
FREEZE MY MIND

& LEAVE ME SHIVERING
IN ICE COLD SILENCE

SINCE YOU LEFT

ALL THE COLOUR
HAS DRAINED

FROM MY LIFE
SINCE YOU LEFT

LEAVING ME
TO LANGUISH

IN THIS TRANSPARENT
WORLD OF ISOLATION

WHERE DID ALL THE LOVE GO?

WHERE DID ALL THE LOVE GO?
WHATEVER HAPPENED TO US

THE GLINT IN OUR EYES
THE LOOK OF LOVE, THE SIGHS

SAYING WORDS LIKE 'I LOVE YOU'
IN LETTERS AND CARDS

WHY DID IT ALL END IN SADNESS
IT DOESN'T MAKE SENSE, THIS MADNESS

ALL THAT PASSION AND DEEP DEVOTION
STARRY SKIES AND SLEEPY OCEANS

OUR FAVOURITE SONG THAT MELTED OUR HEARTS
OUR FAVOURITE MOVIE THAT TORE US APART

LOOKING AT THE STARS AND MAKING WISHES
THOSE MOONLIT MOUTH WATERING

LINGERING KISSES
ALL THAT STEAMY HOT HORNY SEX

GROANING & MOANING
IN THAT DEEP FOREST GRASS

OH! WHERE DID IT AL GO WRONG?
A LOVE THAT WAS CAST IN STONE

LOVE IS LIKE A CANDLE

GROWING WHEN IT'S GLOWING

INTENSIFYING WHEN IT'S BURNING

FAULTERING WHEN IT'S FLICKERING

SIMMERING WHEN IT DIMMERS

ENDED WHEN IT'S EXTINGUISHED

MELANCHOLIC WHEN IT'S MELTED

CONSCIENCE

IN THE MORNING
I LIE HERE QUITE SILENT
LISTENING TO
THE DISTANT PASSING CARS

& THE FARAWAY, FADING SOUND
OF CHILDRENS LAUGHTER
& YOU ARE ON MY MIND
YOUR PRESENCE IS ALL AROUND ME

AT NIGHTFALL
I LIE HERE IN COLD QUIESCENCE
LISTENING TO THE BLACK NIGHT'S SILENCE
& THE DISTANT PASSING TRAINS

AND YOU ARE STILL ON MY MIND
YOUR PRESENCE
SURROUNDS ME
OVERWHELMS ME

ALL DAY AT WORK
YOU ARE STILL WITH ME
EVERYWHERE I GO YOU FOLLOW ME
HAUNTING ME, TAUNTING ME

WHEREVER I GO
WHEREVER I AM
WHEREVER I BE
YOUR SPIRIT-LIKE PRESENCE

WILL BE WITH ME
POSSESSING MY EXISTENCE
UNTIL IT EVENTUALLY TAKES OVER
AND FORMULATES A CO-EXISTENCE

IT'S OVER

WHEN YOU HEAR THOSE WORDS
"WE HAVE TO TALK –
I'LL PUT THE KETTLE ON"
- IT'S TIME TO WALK

IS SILENCE GOLDEN?

DON'T FORGET
IT'S THE WORDS WE DON'T SAY

RATHER THAN THE WORDS WE DO SAY
THAT WE SOMETIMES REGRET

& WE HAVE TO LIVE WITH THAT

IF ONLY

IF ONLY – I COULD MAKE YOU LOVE ME
THE WAY YOU LOVED ME BEFORE

IF ONLY – I COULD RE-KINDLE YOUR FIRE
THAT USED TO BLAZE WITH AWE

IF ONLY – I COULD HAVE THREE WISHES
THREE WISHES – THREE LITTLE WORDS FROM YOU

THREE LITTLE WORDS THAT MEAN SO MUCH
MAY MEAN SO LITTLE TO YOU

YOU ARE THE LOVELIEST GIRL IV'E EVER LOVED
MY ANGEL, AND EVER HAD THE PLEASURE TO MEET

JUST TO HEAR YOU SAY I LOVE YOU 'ONCE MORE –
WOULD MAKE MY LIFE COMPLETE

MISS YOU
(PLEASE COME BACK)

CAUGHT IN THE POSSESSION
OF YOUR PHOTOGRAPH

A SAD LONELY TEAR
ROLLS DOWN MY CHEEK

AS I THINK OF YOU

NOT COMING BACK?

THE BED LIES EMPTY
WHERE YOU ONCE SLEPT

A GHOSTLY SHAPE
SCULPTURED OUT OF SHEETS UNKEPT

A LONELY TATTERED TEDDY
LOOKING LOST AND FOLORN

MY LIFE MEANS NOTHING SINCE
YOU'VE BEEN GONE

SEA OF HEARTBREAK

FOR YOU
I WILL WAIT UNTIL
THE TIDE COMES IN
SO I CAN DROWN IN MY SORROWS

WHEN THE TIDE TURNS

IS WHEN
THE **HEARTBREAKER**
BECOMES THE **HEARTBROKEN**

SEAGULL'S SNACKIN'

WHERE FOR ART THOU?

I HAVE LOVED
AND BEEN LOVED

SO MANY TIMES BEFORE
BUT I CAN'T SEEM TO FIND

THAT SPECIAL LOVE
I'M FOREVER LOOKING FOR?

INCOMPLETE

MY JIGSAW
HAS ONE PIECE MISSING?

THE ONE PIECE
THAT IS YOU!

WE HAVE MOVED ON

MY EYES ARE TIRED
MY FACE LOOKS SAD
FEELING EXPIRED
I RETIRE TO MY BED

TO DREAM -
OF ALL THOSE FUN,
LOVING, HAPPY TIMES
WE SHARED TOGETHER

AND YET NOTHING,
NOTHING EVER LASTS
& IT FEELS LIKE THAT WE
NEVER EVER CARED FOR EACH OTHER

NOW WE HAVE MOVED ON
WE ACT LIKE SISTER & BROTHER
& I TRULY MISS YOU,
MISS YOU AS MY LOVER

ERASURE

SHE'S FADING FROM MY LIFE
FADING FAST
FADING FAST
FADING

SHE'S FADING FROM MY MIND
FADING FAST
FADING FAST
FADING

SHE'S FADING FROM MY MEMORY
FADING FAST
FADING FAST
FADING

SHE'S DISAPPEARING
SHE'S DISAPPEARING
DISAPPEARING

SHE'S GOING
SHE'S GOING
SHE'S GONE

FADED OUT
FADED
FADED

FADED FROM MY MIND
FADED FROM MY MEMORY
FADED FROM MY TIME

THE YAWNING TREE

THE SILVER BIRCH TREE YAWNS
BOUGHS OUTSTRETCHED

GENTLY SHAKES OFF
THE LAST LEAVES OF AUTUMN

STANDING THERE
ALMOST BARK - NAKED

SHIVERING & DITHERING
WAITING PATIENTLY FOR SPRING

STILL LIFE

A PARADE OF PINES STAND STARK
AGAINST THE STEEL GREY SKY

THE NATURALNESS OF NATURE
SEDUCES MY SENSES & STIMULATES MY EYE

& ON THIS SLIME GREEN, COLD, CRISP & BRISK DAY

IN MY MINDS EYE, I PORTRAY
THE STILL, SAD, SILENT, SEASON OF DECAY

ROOTS

THESE ARE THE ROOTS
THE VEINS & SINEWS
OF NATURES LIFEBLOOD
UNEARTHED & EXPOSED
DEEP, DEEP IN THE WOOD

MOTHER NATURE AGENTS

THE TREES HAVE EARS
THE TREES HAVE EYES
THEY WERE PLANTED
ON EARTH
AS SPECIAL
BRANCH SPIES

58

LIMBS

ENTANGLED & MANGLED
TWISTED & CONTORTED
SNAGGED & GNARLED

BRANCHES & BOUGHS
LIKE BROKEN BONES
BARK NAKED & BARE

REACHING OUT
AS IF IN DESPAIR
FOR MOTHER NATURE TO REPAIR

AUTUMN BREEZE

THE SHIVERING GRASS
THE SWAYING TREES

THE FREE FALLING LEAVES
GO WHIRLING, SWIRLING &
DANCING

TO THE WIND WHISTLING
CONCERTO
OF THIS COLD AUTUMN BREEZE

SEASONS TO BE CHEERFUL

ON I GO
INTO THE BALMY BREEZE
THROUGH A WILD WINDY NIGHT
GUSTY GALES & SWAYING TREES

ON I GO
TRUDGING THROUGH
THE DRIVING SNOW
BLACK ICED PAVEMENTS

ON I GO
THROUGH THE RIP ROARING RAIN
FROST FREEZING FOG
INTO THE SCORCHING HOT SUN

THEN BACK AGAIN

CONTRAST

BRRR!!! A COLD, SHARP
ICY, WINTERS' WIND

TINGLES MY EARS
COLOURS MY NOSE

CHAPS MY LIPS
CHATTERS MY TEETH & FREEZES MY HAIR

CONTRASTING SEASONS
CONTRASTING REASONS

PPHEW!!!
A BLAZING, SIZZLING

SCORCHING HOT
SUMMERS' SUN

BLINDS MY EYES
REDDENS MY NOSE

FRECKLES MY FACE
WHITENS MY TEETH & BLEACHES MY HAIR

CONTRASTING SEASONS
CONTRASTING REASONS

SUNRISE, SUNSET

IS IT NOT
THE SUN
THAT
MAKES
YOU FEEL
SO ALIVE

IS IT NOT
THE SUN
THAT
MAKES
YOU SMILE
& LIVING

SEEM
WORTHWHILE
EVERY ONCE
IN AWHILE
BY IT'S
SHEER

RADIANCE & BRILLIANCE
THEY DON'T MAKE WORDS
BEAUTIFUL ENOUGH
TO PORTRAY
THE SIGNIFICANCE
OF THE SUN'S MAGNIFICENCE

A DAY AT THE SEASIDE

A VAST DESERT OF RIPPLED SAND
ROLLED OUT LIKE A CARPET

ETERNALLY SEARCHING
FOR THE ABSENCE OF THE IRISH SEA

MY WIFE, MYSELF
& LITTLE DAUGHTER
BY THE SEA-SHORE

COLLECTING COCKLESHELLS
BY THE SCORE

AND OUR BABY SON
MAKING HIS DEBUT
WITH HIS BUCKET & SPADE

RUNNING WILD & FREE ACROSS
THIS WIDE OPEN WILDERNESS
INTO TIME & SPACE

ANCIENT WATER

ANCIENT WATER
FLOWING DOWNSTREAM
WASHING AWAY THE YEARS

ANCIENT WATER
FLOWING DOWNSTREAM
WASHING AWAY THE YEARS

ANCIENT WATER
FLOWING DOWNSTREAM
WASHING AWAY THE YEARS

EBBING LIFE ALONG THE WAY
ERODING TIME
FROM DAY TO DAY

SKYSCAPES

UP HIGH – INTO THE STEEL GREY SKY
SCANNING THE SMOKE TRAIL OF A SILVER JET
AS IT SCREAMS & WHISTLES BY

UP HIGH – INTO THAT RAINBOWED SKY
WITH IT'S PRISMATIC ARRAY
CREATING A STUNNING DISPLAY

UP HIGH – SQUINTING INTO THE SKY BLUE SKY
AS THE FLAMING SUN
BLINDS MY EYE

UP HIGH – INTO THE COTTON-WOOLED SKY
OF RAINFILLED CLOUDS
THAT DRIFT SLOWLY BY

UP HIGH – AS THE GRUMBLING SKY
VENTS ITS FURY
WITH A THUNDEROUS REPLY

UP HIGH – STIMULATED BY
THE SPRINKLE OF SNOWFLAKES
THAT FLOAT SOFTLY BY

UP HIGH – INTO THAT FROST FROZEN SKY
AS IT HAILS IT'S STONES
ONTO THE BIRDS THAT FLY

UP HIGH – AS A KITE FLYING
THROUGH THE BLUSTERY SKY
AS IT TWISTS THEN TURNS & TANGLES IN A TREE

UP HIGH – INTO THAT STAR TWINKLED SKY
AS THE DREAMY MOON YAWNS
WITH SLEEP IN IT'S EYE

UP HIGH – INTO THE SUN RISEN SKY
WHEN DUSK TURNS TO DAWN
WE WAKE THE MORN AS A NEW 'SKYSCAPE' IS BORN

JACK FROST
(IT'S OFFICIAL - HAS BEEN MADE REDUNDANT!)

UNFORTUNATELY DUE TO MODERN TECHNOLOGY
I.E. UPVC DOUBLE GLAZING
HE CAN NO LONGER CREATE
THOSE SYMETRIC ARTISTIC PATTERNS

UPON OUR BEDROOM WINDOW PANES
AND GARDEN GATES
COS JACK FROST IS
SIMPLY OUT OF DATE!

OH! HOW HE CRIES OUT
FOR THOSE OL' SASH WINDOWS
WHERE HE BRANDISHED HIS TALENTS
SO MANY YEARS AGO

THOSE STREETS UPON STREETS
OF OL' TERRACED HOUSES
NOW SADLY DEMOLISHED -
FOR MODERN CENTRAL HEATED

UPVC SEMIS & TOWN HOUSES
WITH HIS CONTRACT EXPIRED
HE'S UNOFFICIALLY RETIRED
AND NOW POOR OL' JACK FROST

HAS NOWHERE TO GO
COS HIS CRAFT,
HIS EXPERTISE
IS SADLY PASSE & NO MORE

WINTER NYMPH

WAS IS YOU,
WINTER NYMPH?

WHO MADE LOVE TO THE SNOWMAN
& MELTED HIS PRESENCE?

WHO SPRINKLED SAND
ON THAT LITTLE BOY'S SLIDE

WHO THREW STONE SNOWBALLS
AT THE SALVATION ARMY BRASS BAND

WHO DEFROSTED
JACK FROST

WHO THREW ICICLES
AT THE LOCAL WINTER FLASHERMAN

WHO REMOVED THE 'DANGER THIN ICE' SIGN
FROM THE PARK'S ICE SKATING POND

AND WINTER NYMPH,
WAS IT YOU?

WHO RAN NAKED AROUND PICCADILLY CIRCUS
CAUSING COMPLETE CHAOS & NUMEROUS DAMAGE

TO THE SKIDDING CARS & BUSES
UP TO TWO MILES LONG - WELL!

METEOROLOGICAL WEDDING

INBETWEEN THE THUNDER & LIGHTNING –
I PROPOSED
– FOR BETTER WEATHER OF COURSE!

YOU ACCEPTED
INSTANTLY THE SUN CAME OUT
& SMILED UPON US

AS THE CLOUDS DRIFTED DEJECTEDLY AWAY
WE RODE ON A RAINBOW
TO OUR METEOROLOGICAL WEDDING

REFLECTION

WOKE UP ONE MORNING
LOOKED IN THE MIRROR

I SAW A FACE
THAT WASN'T ME?

I CLOSED MY EYES
LOOKED ONCE AGAIN

WHO WAS THIS FACE
LOOKING AT ME?

A FACE FROM THE PAST
A FACE FROM THE FUTURE

A FACE UNFAMILIAR TO ME
SO I WENT BACK TO BED

AND BURIED MY HEAD
'COS I JUST COULDN'T FACE THE DAY

STILL WATERS RUN DEEP

SOMETIMES I WOULD PREFER
TO BE A LITTLE SHALLOW THAN DEEP

SIMPLY BECAUSE IT'S MUCH EASIER
TO SWIM IN SHALLOW WATERS

THAN DROWN IN THE DEEP!

BARRICADES

WHICH WAY SHOULD I GO -
THIS WAY! – THAT WAY
I DON'T KNOW?

TAKEN A WRONG TURNING
ALONG THE WAY
LIFE'S ONE DELAY AFTER DELAY

LOST IN THE DISTANCE
NEED YOUR ASSISTANCE
PLEASE HELP ME ON MY WAY

TAKE ME THROUGH
THE BARRICADES
OF LIFE'S HIGHWAY

CORRIDORS

WALKING DOWN THE CORRIDORS OF LIFE
THROUGH THE PASSAGEWAYS OF TIME

TAKEN THE RIGHT TURNING
SOMETIMES THE WRONG

OPENED THE RIGHT DOORS
SOMETIMES THE WRONG

MADE THE RIGHT DECISIONS
MANY THE WRONG

FOLLOWING THE RIGHT DIRECTIONS
TO MEET THE WRONG CONNECTIONS

CHOSEN THE RIGHT PATH
TO MEET OUR DESTINATION

WALKING DOWN THE CORRIDORS OF LIFE
THROUGH THE PASSAGEWAYS OF TIME

THE ENIGMA
(OF THE SUBCONSCIOUS)

WHAT IS THERE TO FIND?
SEEKING THE SUBCONSCIOUS MIND

STRANGE PHENOMENON
BEYOND OBSCURITY YOU'LL FIND

ALL THE ANSWERS HIDDEN
ALL THE QUESTIONS BLIND

WHAT IS THERE TO FIND?
SEEKING THE SUBCONSCIOUS MIND

ENIGMATIC MYSTERIOUS
YOU'LL FIND

ALL THE ANSWERS HIDDEN
ALL THE QUESTIONS BLIND

WHAT IS THERE TO FIND?
SEEKING THE SUBCONSCIOUS MIND

UNKNOWN TO ALL MANKIND

INTENSE MOMENTS

EVERY SECOND
OF EVERY MINUTE

A CHILD IS BORN
A MARRIAGE HAS BEEN SECURED

A REACHING OF ORGASM HAS OCCURRED
A DEATH IS BEING MOURNED

INTENSE IS THE MOMENT
INTENSE IS THE FEELING

MOMENTS OF GOOD NEWS
MOMENTS OF BAD NEWS

MOMENTS OF HAPPINESS
MOMENTS OF SADNESS

INTENSE ARE THE MOMENTS
INTENSE ARE THE FEELINGS

OF YOUR EXISTENCE
OF YOUR BEING & YOUR SUBSISTENCE

THE TRAGIC DEATH OF AMANDA JANE

IT WAS HER EARLY ENVIROMENT
THAT HAD AFFECTED HER
NEGLECTED BY HER MOTHER,
HER FATHER SHE HAD NEVER SEEN

BORN A BASTARD, A MISTAKE
WHATEVER WAS SHOULD NEVER HAVE BEEN
FROM BOARDING SCHOOLS TO REMAND HOMES
THEY COULDN'T UNDERSTAND HER – POOR AMANDA

PORTRAYED AS A REBEL,
AN OUTCAST
SHE KEPT RUNNING AWAY,
WHERE COULD SHE STAY?

NOBODY LOVED HER, NOBODY LIKED HER
NOBODY CARED FOR – POOR AMANDA
REJECT BY SOCIETY, WHO COULD SHE TURN TO,
WHO'S THERE TO GUIDE HER

WHAT IS LIFE WITHOUT LOVE & CARE?
 - A GARDEN WITHOUT FLOWERS
A DAMAGED MIND THAT WILL NEVER MEND
SHE HAD NO CHANCE, NO HOPE, NO FRIEND

HER THOUGHTS TURNED TO ACID
A DESPAIRING FIGHT WITH HER NARCOTIC MIND
NOTHING TO LOSE ONLY TIME
THEN TIME CAME LIKE A FRIEND

AND CARRIED HER TO THE BITTER END
A TRAGEDY SHE DIES, SO SAD SHE LIES
BETRAYED BY YOU & I - THE SO CALLED CARING
HUMANITARIAN SOCIETY WE CALL MANKIND

FAITH 1965 (my first ever poem!)

YOU'VE GOT TO HAVE FAITH IN THE LORD
HE HAS FAITH IN YOU
HE MADE THE WORLD
AND HE MADE IT JUST FOR YOU

I KNOW YOU MY FRIEND HAVE SINNED MANY TIMES
& THE LORD KNOWS THAT TOO
BUT NEVER LOOK DOWN ALWAYS LOOK UP
BECAUSE HE STILL HAS FAITH IN YOU

& IF YOU HAVE FAITH IN THE LORD
CONFESS THE WRONG YOU DO
LOVE ALL OTHERS & THEY'LL LOVE YOU
BE FAITHFUL MY FRIEND & ALWAYS BE TRUE

& NOW YOU HAVE FAITH IN THE LORD
HE HAS FORGIVEN YOU
FROM THE DAY YOU LIVE 'TIL THE DAY YOU DIE
HE'LL ALWAYS HAVE FAITH IN YOU

YES, FAITH IS THAT WORD
THAT WORD HE GAVE TO YOU

WHY DO WE?

WHY DO WE LOVE
WHY DO WE HATE
WHY DO WE
FROM BEING BORN DETERIOATE

WHY DO WE LAUGH
WHY DO WE CRY
WHY DO WE LIVE
WHY DO WE DIE

WHY DO WE –
FOR WHAT
FOR WHO
FOR WHY?

WHAT ON EARTH?

HAVIN' HAD ENOUGH OF IT ALL ONE DAY
I WENT ON A 'GETAWAYFROMITALL'
TYPE PACKAGE HOLIDAY

BETTER KNOWN FOR BEING A BIT OF A LUNE
I CHARTERED A ROCKET
AND FLEW TO THE MOON

LANDED
'BY THE LIGHT OF THE SILVERY MOON'
BESIDE THE 'SEA OF TRANQUILITY'

LISTENING TO PINK FLOYD'S
'THE DARK SIDE OF THE MOON'
ON MY MP PLAYER

BUT AFTER HAVIN' A 'GRAND DAY OUT' UP HERE
I GOT A LITTLE CHEESED OFF
DUE TO THE LACK OF ATMOSPHERE

THEN ONE DAY
A CERTAIN 'MAN IN THE MOON'
LET ME KNOW

THAT THERE WAS
A TOTAL ECLIPSE ON THE WAY
AND THAT I'D BETTER LEAVE REAL SOON

SO I CONTACTED GROUND CONTROL
FOR MY CHARTERED ROCKET
WITH NOTHING BUT MOONDUST IN MY POCKET

I EVENTUALLY LANDED IN A GRASSY MEADOW
AND AWOKE TO THE SOUND OF
CAT STEVENS 'MOONSHADOW'

GIMME SHELTER

ON BUNKERS HILL, UP DAISY NOOK,
IN FAILSWORTH. MANCHESTER
I DUG MYSELF A NUCLEAR HIDE OUT

AND FALL OUT SHELTER
WITH TWO FOOT THICK CONCRETE TRENCHES
ELECTRONICALLY OPERATED CURTAINS

INFRA RED LIGHTING, A STANDBY GENERATOR
FILTRATION ROOM WITH PLENTY OF WENCHES
I,OOO GALLON UNDERGROUND WATER TANK

FOR MY HOMEBREW KIT – IT LOOKS REALLY SWANK!
I'D SIT BY MY MASTER CONTROL
CLICKING ON & OF THE GARDEN FLOODLIGHTS

& HAVE HIDDEN SENSORS TO DETECT
UNWELCOME VISITORS LIKE
DOUBLE GLAZING SALESMEN,

JEOVAH'S WITNESSES
& OTHER SUCH PREDATORS
WITH HD BLUE RAY 60" CINEMA SCREEN

AND ALLROUND SURROUND SOUND HI FI SYSTEM
(STATE OF THE ART – I MEAN!)
WITH A RACK OF D,V,D'S & A STACK OF C,D'S

AN 'I-POD' & AN 'I PHONE' - I'M NOT HARD TO PLEASE!
READY FOR ACTION & READY FOR REACTION
SO BRING ON THE WEAPONS OF MASS DESTRUCTION

SALT OF THE EARTH

HE WAS A SALT OF THE EARTH TYPE GUY
A REAL DIAMOND GEEZER, TOP MAN

JACK THE LAD, RUM OL' BUGGER
GREAT GUY, GOOD LAUGH

SUPER STAR, SHINING LIGHT
A LADIES MAN ABOUT THE TOWN - THE MAN

UNTIL THE DAY HE STEPPED OUT OF LINE
AND LET THE SIDE DOWN

WHEN HE CONFESSED TO BE
A CLOSET, CHEESY WESTLIFE FAN!

ODE TO THE ASHTRAY

TO ALL YOU SMOKERS I CAN SAFELY SAY –
GET YOUR FAG ENDS OUT OF MY TRAY
'COS I'M OFFICIALLY FAGLESS & FREE
NO MORE SMOKIN' IN PUBS – YOU SEE

I AM NOW OBSOLETE
JUST A POLISHED ORNAMENT TO GREET
& GLAD TO SAY THAT I'M NOT TO BE
STUBBED OUT OR PUT OUT IN ANYWAY

I HAVE FULFILLED MY USEFULNESS
IT'S FAG ASHES TO ASHES,
DUST TO DUST
ALL YOU SMOKERS CAN ALL GET LOST

SO JUST 'BUTT' OUT CHUM
WITH YOUR SPAT OUT NUTS OR STICKY GUM
JUST LEAVE ME TO REST IN PEACE
'COS IT'S 'TIME GENTLEMEN PLEASE!!'

DOWN MEMORY LAME

"CAN YOU SEE '*THINGYMIJIG*' OVER THERE
YOU KNOW '*OOJIMACALLIT*'?
    -    "

"OH! '*WHATSISNAME*?'– YOU MEAN?"
"YES '*OOJIT?*' WITH HIS '*THINGYMIBOB*' ON"

"HE LOOKS A RIGHT '*SO & SO?*' –
HOLD ON HERE COMES OL' '*DOOINS?*'

'ON HIS '*WHATNOT?*'
I THINK HIS MEMORY'S GONE YOU KNOW" -

"YES – I THINK SO TOO –
LET'S GO TO ERM '*YOU KNOW WHO'S*'?

DOWN '*HOWDOYOUSAYIT*'
-OH! IT'S ON THE TIP OF MI TONGUE"

BEGINNING WITH M? SOMETHING
BLOODY HELL! LANE!"

OWD JIM

"DID I EVER TELL YAH KID",
SAID OWD JIM, LOOKING GRIM
- "BOUT TH'TIME I TRIED TO COMMIT SUICIDE? –
WIFE LEFT ME, UNITED LOST CUP,
TORIES GORR IN - GOD FORBID!

AN' TO TOP IT ALL –
IT WERE A CITY FAN SHE BUGGERED OFF WIV!
AYE! LADDIE T'WAS ON BANKS OF 'RIVER IRWELL'
I STOOD,
GAZIN' INTO THAT MURKY LOOKIN' MUD –

THEN I SAID TO MYSEL' –
JIM!! MEK IT WORTHWHILE
GO OUT IN DIGNITY & IN STYLE –
YAH! SEE KID - I COULN'T SEE MYSEL' ONE BIT
FLOATIN' ABOUT IN ALL THAT SHIT!

SO T'WAS OFF TO RAILWAY LINES IN
SHEER DESPERATION,
SOMEHOW I ARRIVED AT
'NEWT'NEATH TRAIN STATION'
& BUMPED INTO 'JOE SMYTHE' TH' RAILWAY POET

WHO CONVINCED ME,
SO POETICALLY NOT TO DO IT
- BUT AFTER READING HIS BOOK
I WISHED I HAD –
I CURSED MY LUCK!

SO BACK TO 'OWDHAM ROAD
WITHOUT MUCH ADO & FUSS
I DECIDED TO THROW MYSEL'
UNDER THE '98 BUS'
BUT TYPICAL OF MI DESTINY & FATE

- THE BLOODY THING TURNED UP LATE!
WELL LADDIE! I THOWT,
WHERE DO I GO FROM 'ERE -
TO PICCADILLY GARDENS TO SET MYSEL' ON FEER!
OR THROW MYSEL' OFF TH' C.I.S. –

BUT THERE AGEN KID –
JUST THINK OF TH' MESS
WHAT ABOUT GAS OVEN
OR AN OVERDOSE
PLASTIC BAG O'ER YED, I SUPPOSE

THEN I THOWT SOD IT! –
'HARI-KARI'S' NOT FER ME
THERE'S PLENTY MORE FISH IN TH'SEA -
AN' THERE'S SURE TO BE –
A LITTLE TIDDLER LEFT FER ME?

AN' I CAN PUT UP WI TORIES POLICIES
OF NO SENSE & REASON
AN' AS FER BLOODY UNITED -
THERE'S ALWAYS
NEXT BLOODY SEASON!".

NOW WE'RE GERRIN' OWDER

NOW WE'RE GERRIN' OWDER
AN' OUR KID'S
HAVE ALL GOT WED
LYIN' HERE PONDERIN'
HALF A SLEEP IN THIS OL' BED
OF TIME'S GONE BYE & BYE
WHEN WE STILL HAD THAT TWINKLE IN TH'EYE

NOW WE'RE GERRIN' OWDER
AN' OUR BED'S A LITTLE WORN & TATTERED
WITH ALL THOSE PAST NIGHT'S OF
UNBRIDLED LOVE & PASSION
AS OUR THREADBARE,
LUKEWARM BOTTOM'S REFLECT ON
WHEN LOVE MEKIN' WAS THE FASHION

NOW WE'RE GERRIN' OWDER
FADED MEMORIES A LIFE-TIME AWAY
AS WE GERR UP TO GRACE TH' DUTIFUL DAY
ME IN TH' GARDEN POTTERIN'
'BOUT TH' POTTIN SHED
YOU KNITTIN' BY TH' FIRE
OR MEKIN' 'OLE' MEAL BREAD

NOW WE'RE GERRIN' OWDER
AS TH' SEXPERT'S SAY -
'TH' MIND IS WILLIN-
BUT TH'FLESH IS WEAK'
LYIN' HERE IN TH' BED
THAT USED TO SQUEAK

NOW WE'RE GERRIN' OWDER
WI' ME IN COMB'S AN' BEDSOCK'S
YOU IN OL' WOOLY VEST
WI TEETH IN TH' JAR – CHATTERIN' AWAY IN JEST
AS WE RETIRE TO OUR WORN & CLAPPED OUT BED
BUT NOT FER MEKIN' LOVE - NOR US - OH! NO!
- WE'D SOONER MEK' TEA INSTEAD

THE DON'T MEK' 'UM
LIKE THEY USED TO

THEY DON'T MAKE CHIPS LIKE THEY USED TO
DONE IN BEST BEEF DRIPPING
SCOOPED IN NEWSPAPER WRAPPING
TASTING LIKE THEY USED TO

THEY DON'T MAKE BREAD LIKE THEY USED TO
LIKE LITTLE HOVIS LOAVES
SPREAD WITH HUGH FAY'S SLAB BUTTER
TASTING LIKE THEY USED TO

THEY DON'T MAKE MOVIES LIKE THEY USED TO
WITH HAPPY ENDINGS –
WHEN THE GOOD GUY GETS THE GIRL
JUST LIKE THEY USED TO

THEY DON'T HAVE NEIGHBOURS LIKE THEY USED TO
WI' FRONT DOORS OPEN WIDE
TO WELCOME YOU INSIDE
WITH GREAT COMMUNITY SPIRIT & PRIDE
JUST LIKE THEY USED TO

THEY DON'T MAKE MUSIC LIKE THEY USED TO
WITH THE BIG BAND SOUNDS
& PROPER BALLROOM DANCIN' AROUND
LIKE WE USED TO

THEY DON'T MAKE LOVE LIKE THEY USED TO
NOT UNTIL YOU GOT WED
THEN IT WAS OFF TO TH' BRIDAL BED
WI' GOOD MORALS & RESPECT LIKE THEY HAD TO

YESTERDAY'S HERO

IT SEEMS LIKE ONLY YESTERDAY
WHEN HEADS TURNED MY WAY

WHEN I WAS YOUNG & EASY ON THE EYE
THE GIRLS USED TO TURN THEIR HEADS & SMILE

WHEN THEY PASSED ME BY
WITH A CHEEKY WINK OF AN EYE

THE DAY'S WHEN I WAS TRENDY & COOL
A BIT OF A LOOKER - A RIGHT RUM BUGGER

BUT OH! HOW THINGS CRUELLY CHANGE
WHEN FATHER TIME

CATCHES UP ON YOU
NOW I FEEL LIKE SOME KIND OF FOOL

A YESTERDAY'S HERO
A FALLEN STAR

PAST MY SELL BY DATE
HOW DID I GET INTO THIS PITIFUL STATE?

OBSOLETE, OUTMODED & OUT OF DATE
YES, I REMEMBER WHEN HEADS TURNED MY WAY

NOW THEY TURN,
TURN SADLY AWAY

REWIND

WHO'S FAST FORWARDED MY LIFE
I WANT IT REWINDING BACK
TO MY ILLUSTRIOUS PAST
WHEN I WAS AT MY HAPPIEST
& BREATHTAKING BEST

I WANT IT REWINDING
BACK TO MY PAST TO ERASE
ALL THE BAD THINGS IN MY LIFE
THE STUPID MISTAKES
THE HEARTBREAKS & PAIN

& PLAY OVER & OVER
THE HAPPY MOMENTS
THE GOOD TIMES
OF MY LIFE
OVER & OVER & OVER AGAIN

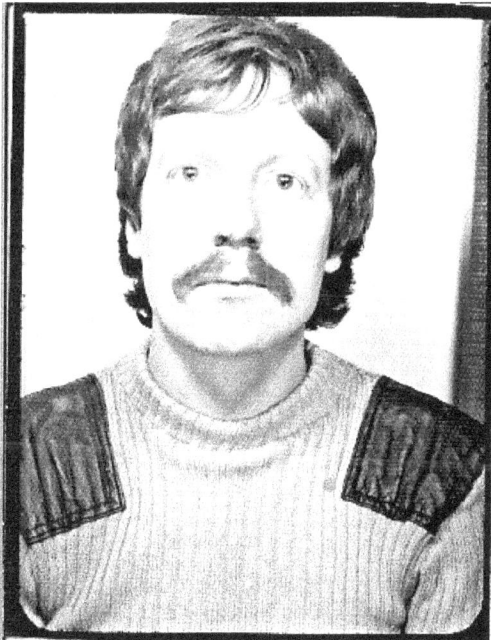

PET HATES

TREADING IN DOG POO
SQUISHING A SLUG
OR A SNEAKY STONE INSIDE YOUR SHOE

SWALLOWING FAT
OR CHEWING GRISTLE
AN ANNOYING GUY WITH A TUNELESS WHISTLE

SWEATY FEET AND SMELLY PITS
JORDAN TYPE BIMBOS
WITH SILICONE T*ITS

UNEXPECTED SNOTTY SNEEZES
MESSED UP HAIR
BY EVIL WINDS AND BREEZES

LOW-LIFE IGNORANT SCUMMY YOBS
HIGH-LIFE ARROGANT
SMARMY SNOBS

MUFFIN TOPPED GIRLS
WITH SCRUNCHED UP HAIR
WITH LOTS OF KIDS – LIVING ON WELFARE

PEE-SOAKED SEATS IN DIRTY GENTS
LATCHES MISSING OFF TOILET DOORS
& BAD SPELLING GRAFFITTI ON THE WALLS

STALE SMOKED CLOTHES
THAT GETS IN MY HAIR
& GETS UP RIGHT MY NOSE

DRIBBLING MILKY CEREAL DOWN YOUR CHIN
FAG-ASHED KISSES
GETS UNDER MY SKIN

A SNEAKY COLD SORE ON YOUR LIP
A SUDDEN FLY IN THE EYE
OR CATCHING YOUR WILLY IN YOUR ZIP

RIP OFF TAXIS
FOWL MOUTHED
LADISH LASSES

BOY RACERS PLAYING LOUD RAP
FROM SPEEDING CARS –
NEED A GOOD SLAP!

B.T. AUTOMATED TELEPHONE CALLS
TOMCATS SPRAYING
ON YOUR GARAGE DOORS

TIGHT-WADS
WHO DON'T BUY NEWSPAPERS
BUT READ THE PRINT OFF YOURS

THE POST OFFICE QUEUE
READERS DIGEST SAYING YOU'VE WON £10,000 –
THIS COULD BE YOU!

PEOPLE WHO CONSTANTLY WHINE & WHINGE
UNWITTY CHANTS FROM MORONIC
FOOTY FANS - MAKES ME CRINGE

AS CUTTING YOUR FINGER ON CORNED BEEF TINS
PEOPLE WHO TALK BUT NEVER LISTEN
LIKE – SELF OPINIONATED POLITICAL CRETINS

VICIOUS DOGS AND OWNERS ALIKE
IDIOTS WHO HAVE
NO LIGHTS ON THEIR BIKES

A SNAPPED SHOELACE
WHEN YOU'RE
IN A MAD RACE

AN INTRUDING ZIT ON THE END OF YER NOSE
BEING ATTACKED BY A THORN
WHEN YOU PRUNE A ROSE

HURTFUL, TACKLESS PILLOCKS
WHO HAVE THE AUDACITY TO CRITICISE
THESE I REALLY HATE & DESPISE

THAT SONG REMINDS ME

THAT SONG REMINDS ME OF A CERTAIN TIME IN LIFE
WHEN LIFE WAS CAREFREE, FULL & NEVER DULL
WITH LOTS OF LOVE AND PASSION
WHEN MINI SKIRTS WERE THE FASHION

THE CHILDISH TEENAGE FUN AND LAUGHTER
THOSE WILD PARTIES, THE FAIRS AND CARNIVALS
ROCK CONCERTS AND FESTIVALS
CAMPING, FULL OF PRANKS AND DARES

DANCING, PRANCING AND SINGING ALOUD
THOSE S'EXCITING SUMMER HOLS.
WITH THE IN CROWD
GORGEOUS GIRLFRIENDS AND GREAT MATES
HANGING AROUND THE COUNCIL ESTATES

WHEN SUMMER SEEMED SO LONG
OH! HOW THE TIME HAS FLOWN
BUT I ALWAYS REMEMBER
WHEN I HEAR THAT SONG

THAT SONG REMINDS ME OF A CERTAIN TIME IN LIFE
WHEN LIFE WAS CAREFREE, FULL & NEVER DULL
LOTS OF LOVE AND PASSION
WHEN MINI SKIRTS WERE THE FASHION

WITH GREAT MUSIC, CLUBS AND DANCE HALLS
THOSE SLEEPY, MIDNIGHT MOVIES
WHERE WE SNOGGED' IN THE STALLS
FALLING IN LOVE & OUT OF LOVE AGAIN

GROPING THE GIRLS BEHIND THE BACKYARD WALLS
BEING CHASED DOWN THE BACK ENTRIES
BY IRATE MUMS AND DADS
YES, THOSE WERE THE DAYS I CAN RECALL

THE WORLD IS MY HOME
(song)

OH! I'M JUST TRAVELLING ON
JUST ME THE AIR AND THE SUN
SEEKING ADVENTURE, EXCITEMENT AND FUN

ANY DIRECTION FOR ME
JUST AS LONG AS I'M FREE
TO GO STROLLING AND RAMBLING ALONG

OH! I'M JUST TRAVELLING ON
JUST ME THE AIR AND THE SUN
SEEKING ADVENTURE EXCITEMENT AND FUN

I'll GO OVER THE MOUNTAINS, HILLS AND UPLANDS
THROUGH THE FORESTS, HEATHS AND WOODLANDS
DOWN THE VALLEYS, DALES AND
LOWLANDS

I'LL ROW THE RIVERS
SAIL THE SEAS
TO ANY COUNTRY I PLEASE

FROM THE U.S.A. TO BOTANY BAY
I'LL FIND MY WAY
'COS I'M HAPPY JUST TO BE ON MY OWN

OH! I'M JUST TRAVELLING ON
JUST ME THE AIR AND THE SUN
SEEKING ADVENTURE, EXCITEMENT & FUN

IT'S GOODBYE TO THE RAT-RACE BACK HOME
I'M OFF TO VENTURE AND ROAM
NO MORE WORRIES FOR ME, NO MORE MISERY

'COS I'M HAPPY JUST TO BE ON MY OWN
JUST ME THE AIR AND THE SUN
SEEKING ADVENTURE, EXCITEMENT AND FUN

ANY DIRECTION FOR ME
JUST AS LONG AS I'M FREE
TO GO STROLLING AND RAMBLING ALONG

PICCADILLY 2 a.m.

PICCADILLY 2 A.M.

AND THE TOWN'S CRAWLING WITH DRUNKEN MEN,
WINO'S, GIN SOAKER'S, GAY LIBERATOR'S

DROP OUT'S, JUNKIE'S, CHINESE WAITER'S,
TRAMP'S, VAGRANT'S, PIMP'S AND WHORE'S

ALL MISGUIDED,
ALL OFF COURSE

GOING NOWHERE, NOWHERE TO GO, GOING ALONE
GOING NOWHERE, NOWHERE TO GO, GOT NO HOMES

PICCADILLY GARDENS 3 A.M.

THE BENCHES ARE LITTERED WITH DRUNKEN MEN,
WINO'S, GIN SOAKER'S, GAY LIBERATOR'S,

DROP OUT'S, JUNKIE'S, CHINESE WAITER'S,
TRAMP'S, VAGRANT'S, PIMP'S AND WHORE'S

TRAGIC PEOPLE, LONELY PEOPLE,
ALL MISGUIDED, ALL OFF COURSE

GOING NOWHERE, NOWHERE TO GO, GOING ALONE
GOING NOWHERE, NOWHERE TO GO, GOT NO HOMES

BOOTLE STEET 6 A.M.

THE CELLS ARE FULL WITH DRUNKEN MEN,
WINO'S, GIN SOAKER'S, GAY LIBERATOR'S,

DROP OUT'S, JUNKIE'S, CHINESE WAITER'S,
TRAMP'S, VAGRANT'S, PIMP'S AND WHORE'S

FOUND SOMEWHERE, SOMEWHERE TO GO,
NOT ALONE

FOUND SOMEWHERE, SOMEWHERE TO GO,
GOT NEW HOMES

CHAMELEON

I'VE BEEN A SOCIOLOGY STUDENT,
A VEGAN & SMOKED POT
BOUGHT DINGY CLOTHES FROM
JUMBLE SALES & THE LOCAL OXFAM SHOP

CAMPAIGNED FOR
NUCLEAR DISARMAMENT
AGAINST THE TRIDENT MISSILE
AND NEUTRON BOMB

GOT INVOLVED IN DEMOS, RALLIES
& MARCHES - JUST FOR FUN
I'VE BEEN AN ANTI-ESTABLISHMENT, ANTI-RACIST
GAY LIBERATOR, ANTI-SEXIST & ANARCHIST

WENT TO ROCK CONCERTS ABSORBING
SPRINGSTEEN & DYLANESQUE SONGS OF PROTEST
HANDED OUT LEFTWING LEAFLETS,
ADORNED MYSELF WITH C.N.D. BADGES

YES, PLAYING THE RADICAL
WAS MY IDENTITY - UNTIL,
I GRADUATED & ATTAINED MY HONOURS DEGREE
THEN MY NEW IMAGE BECAME IMINENT - YOU SEE

A MERCHANT BANKER I WAS TO BE
ON A RATHER OBESE SALARY
I DONED A PINSTRIPED SMILE
& CLICKING HEEL SHOES

WITH MY 'MICHAEL HESTLETINE' QUIFF
– I COULDN'T LOSE
INVESTED MY MONEY IN STOCKS & SHARES
STUDIED THE 'TIMES INDEX' OF COURSE!

BECAME A WHIZZ KID, A YUPPIE OF HIGH SOCIETY
JOINED THE MASONS BROTHERHOOD & VOTED TORY
HUNG AROUND RATHER NAUGHTILY
THE STOCKBROKERS BELT LAVATORY

AND IF ONE SO HAPPENED TO BE DISCREDITED
THERE WAS ALWAYS
'DADDIES BUSINESS' TO BE INHERITED
SO IT'S GOOD OL' AVARICIOUS OLD BOY ME

A STAUNCH MONETARIST SUPPORTER OF MRS T
WENT TO THE BALLET, THE OPERA & PROMS
JET SET DISCOS & CLUBS
WITH MY HIGH SOCIETY CHUMS

HAD THE OCCASIONAL SNORT OF COKE
& TIPPLE OF VINTAGE
WITH A DEBUTANT IN EACH ARM
BEING A TOP BLOKE– I TOOK FULL ADVANTAGE

DINED WITH ROYALTY,
FILM STARS & ARTISTES
WENT TO MASONIC FUNCTIONS
& SO CALLED ECCENTRIC PARTIES

YOU SEE – THIS WAS THE NEW LIFE FOR ME
STUFF THE UNIONS, THE COMMIES & THE C.N.D.
DOWN WITH THE WORKERS & UP WITH MRS. T
& THERE'S PLENTY MORE LIKE ME IN THE UNIVERSITY

SO ALWAYS BE AWARE
OF CHAMELEONS LIKE ME
WHO'S NOW THINKING
OF JOINING THE S.D.P

POSH GIRLS DON'T SMILE

POSH GIRLS DON'T SMILE THEY SNEER & SNIDE
THEY DON'T THINK IT'S WORTHWHILE TO SMILE

TOO WORKING CLASS, TOO COMMON
PERHAPS THEY ARE TOO PROUND, TOO CONTENT

TOO INTELLIGENT, TOO IMPORTANT TO SMILE
BUT THEY'RE VERY GOOD AT LAUGHING

AT OTHER PEOPLES MISFORTUNES OH! YA!
ORRFF THEY GO WITH THEIR HEADS HELD HIGH

ONTO HIGH HORSES WITH NOSES IN THE AIR
THEY DON'T CARE WHY SHOULD THEY

THEY'RE TOO WRAPPED UP
IN THEIR SELF IMPORTANCE TO CARE

& TO WORRY ABOUT SUCH TRIVIALITIES
LIKE HOW TO SAY THANK YOU & PLEASE

WALKING WITHOUT NOTICING ANYBODY
TALKING WITHOUT LISTENING TO ANYBODY
(EXCEPT WHEN MONEY TALKS)

POSH GIRLS DON'T SMILE, THEY SNEER & SNIDE
THEY DON'T THINK IT'S WORTHWHILE TO SMILE

WHY SHOULD THEY - GOOD MANNERS & COURTESY
ARE OLD FASHIONED ANYWAY

BUT GOOD OLD FASHIONED
WORKING CLASS GIRLS SMILE & WHY?

BECAUSE THEY CAN AFFORD TO, THAT'S WHY
- IT COST NOTHING!

BITTER & TWISTED

WHO ARE THEY?
THOSE FACELESS MEN
THOSE TASTELESS MEN

THOSE HEARTLESS CLOWNS
WHO KEEP YOU DOWN
AND IN YOUR PLACE – IT'S SUCH A DISGRACE

WHO ARE THEY?
THOSE NAMELESS ONES
THOSE BLAMELESS ONES

THOSE MINDLESS MEN
WHO BUILD YOU UP, THEN KNOCK YOU DOWN
& MAKE YOU START ALL OVER AGAIN

WHO ARE THEY?
THOSE SO CALLED EVIL GENIUSES
THOSE PROFITEERS, THOSE RACKETEERS

WHO PULL ALL THE STRINGS
ON POLITICS,
RELIGION AND THINGS

WE ARE SOCIETIES SLAVES
RULED BY ANCIENT LAWS
WE ARE SOCIETIES DOGS – LEAD BY ANCIENT BORES

STILL THE RAT RACE GOES ON
SHIT ON, SPIT ON
ONE BY ONE

WE ARE BEING TAKEN IN
BY THE MEDIA, THE PROPAGANDISTS
WHO BRAINWASH AND CONTROL

THE WAY WE THINK,
THE WAY WE ARE
THE WAY WE STRIVE

BY LIMITING OUR MINDS, OUR INTELLIGENCE, OUR
IMAGINATIONS KEEPING US DIVIDED AND DEPRIVED
SO THAT WE 'LL NEVER EVER GET ANYWHERE IN LIFE

MAYBE WE ARE TOO CONTENT
BT ACCEPTING THE WAY THINGS ARE
BUT CONTENTMENT ISN'T HAPPINESS

IT'S MUCH, MUCH LESS
IT'S SITTING BACK & TAKING ALL THE BULLSHIT
WITHOUT MAKING ANY EFFORT TO DISPUTE IT

WE ARE THE PUPPETS, THE MARIONETTES
FIGHTING AND CONFRONTING OURSELVES
OUR OWN WORST ENEMIES

OUT OF CONTROL, BY BEING CONTROLLED
EXPLOITED, MANIPULATED AND ABUSED
YET WE CANNOT SEE

DEMOCRATIC FREEDOM –
WE ARE ONLY AS FREE
AS WE ARE ALLOWED TO BE

YOU SEE –
WITH ALL THOSE STRINGS ATTACHED
WE'RE NOT REALLY FREE AT ALL!

SO WHERE ARE THEY?
THESE FACELESS MEN
THESE TASTELESS MEN

THESE NAMELESS ONES
THESE BLAMELESS ONES
THESE MINDLESS ONES

COME OUT AND IDENTIFY YOURSELVES
COME OUT AND CONFRONT US
EYE TO EYE, FACE TO FACE, MAN TO MAN

DO YOU NOT HAVE A CONSCIENCE
DO YOU NOT HAVE ANYTHING TO OFFER US
ONLY HARDSHIP, HEARTACHE AND PITY

JUST PASSING THROUGH

'TIME IS OF THE ESSENCE'
IT IS OFTEN SAID
NOT TO BE WASTED IN ANYWAY
LIVING FOR THE MOMENT 'TIL THE END OF YOUR DAY

ALL IS PERMANENTLY TEMPORARY
A WAXED CANDLE FLICKERING
'TIL THE FLAME FLITTERS SLOWLY AWAY
LIFE IS ME, LIFE IS YOU

A MERE CHAPTER
IN THE BOOK OF LIFE
HERE TODAY, GONE TOMORROW
JUST PASSING THROUGH

LIFE'S SO PRECIOUS
A LIVING TREASURE
WITH LOVING MOMENTS TO CHERISH
BUT SADLY NOTHING LASTS FOREVER

A PITY WE HAVE TO PERISH
LIFE IS ME, LIFE IS YOU
HERE TODAY, GONE TOMORROW
JUST PASSING THROUGH

R. I. P.

YOU NEVER KNOW WHEN YOUR TIME'S UP
YOU NEVER KNOW THE DAY
LIFE'S LIKE A GRAND FINALE
IN A STAGED PLAY
AS THE CURTAIN COMES DOWN
& WHISPERS THE END
THIS IS WHEN
YOU GO MY FRIEND
A CANDLE EXTINGUISHED
THE FINAL CHAPTER FINISHED
OFF TO MEET YOUR MAKER
THE DREADED UNDERTAKER

YOUR COFFIN BEING CARRIED
CREMATED OR BURIED?
REST, PRAYERS & TEARS
AFTER THE BUFFET
FUNERAL CAKE, A FEW BEERS
GONE BUT NOT FORGOTTEN
JUST A FADED MEMORY
PLAQUE OR HEADSTONE
WORDS IN THE OBITUARY
ONE OF THE BEST
GONE LIKE THE REST
GONE TO A BETTER PLACE

OUT OF THE RAT RACE
FIGHTING OVER THE WILL
WHO'S PAYING THE FUNERAL BILL
FAMILY FALLEN OUT
WHAT'S IT ALL ABOUT?
LEFT IT TO THE NIECE
HOW COULD YOU
REST IN PEACE
GOOD NIGHT, GOD BLESS
SEE YOU IN THE AFTERLIFE
FROM YOUR IRATE EX-WIFE......

EMPTINESS

WHEN YOU LOSE
SOMEBODY YOU LOVE

TAKE A SORROWFUL
LOOK AT THE HEAVEN ABOVE

SAY A LITTLE PRAYER
LOST IN THOUGHT, DEEP IN DESPAIR

THE FEELINGS YOU HAVE
FOR THOSE WHO YOU CARE

MANY SLEEPLESS NIGHTS
AND DAYDREAMING DAYS

AFTER ALL THE SADNESS AND TEARS
FAST FORWARD ME ON TO THE HEALING YEARS

YOUR LIFE HAS NOW GONE
AND I MUST MOVE ON

BUT I'LL ALWAYS GLANCE BACK
AND I'LL NEVER EVER FORGET

LIFE IS FOR THE LIVING

'EVERY CLOUD HAS A SILVER LINING'
'TOMORROW'S ANOTHER DAY'
EVEN TIME THE GREAT HEALER
WON'T MAKE IT GO AWAY

'GONE TO A BETTER PLACE' – THEY SAY
'IT'S THE BEST WAY TO GO'
'QUICK & WITHOUT PAIN'
- HOW DO THEY KNOW??

YOU NEVER KNOW WHAT'S AROUND THE CORNER
YOU NEVER KNOW YOUR FATE
'SO LET'S MAKE HAY WHILE THE SUN SHINES'
- DON'T LEAVE IT ALL TOO LATE

HERE TODAY & GONE TOMORROW
'LIFE'S TOO SHORT' THEY SAY
SO LET'S MAKE THE BL**DIN' BEST OF IT
& LIVE LIFE FOR TODAY

JIGSAW

HOPE MY LIFE
IS LIKE A JIGSAW PUZZLE

AND WHEN I PUT ALL
THE PIECES TOGETHER

I WOULD BE HAPPY
TO DIE COMPLETE

QUOTATIONS

THE BEST **ADVICE** TO GIVE A PERSON
IS TO LISTEN TO **NO ADVICE** AT ALL

OR TAKE A VERY CLOSE LOOK AT THE PERSON
WHO OFFERS THEIR ADVICE

-

A RAT RACE -
I WOULD RATHER LIVE IN A **RICH** RAT RACE
THAN A **POOR** ONE

OUR **THOUGHTS & IDEAS** CHANGE
LIKE THE **WEATHER**
(WHICH PSYCHOLOGICALLY AFFECTS THE MIND)

ALL **TRADITIONS** ARE PERPETUAL BORES

- -

IT'S THE **PAST** THAT MAKES THE **PRESENT**

- -

SURELY **FANTASY** IS REALITY
AS **DYING** IS PART OF LIVING.

- -

IS **DEATH** THE ONLY **CONCLUSION?**

- -

EVERYTHING THESE DAYS IS
PERMANENTLY TEMPORARY

DAVID PRESTBURY

WAS BORN IN GREAT ANCOATS,
MANCHESTER, ENGLAND
SPENT FIRST TWO YEARS OF HIS LIFE
IN GORTON, MANCHESTER 18

HIS BOYHOOD YEARS IN CLAYTON, (UNTIL 15)
MANCHESTER 11
& THE REST OF HIS TEENAGE YEARS
IN FAILSWORTH, MANCHESTER

HAS LIVED IN BOWKER VALE, WHITEFIELD &
PRESTWICH FOR TWENTY YEARS OR SO
(ALL NORTH MANCHESTER AREAS)
& IS NOW LIVING BACK IN FAILSWORTH,

WAS (UN) EDUCATED AT 'RAVENSBURY STREET',
SEC. SCHOOL IN CLAYTON, MANCHESTER 11
LEFT SCHOOL AT 15
TO BECOME AN APPRENTICE COMPOSITOR
THEN ON TO BE A JOURNEYMAN COMPOSITOR
(LETTERPRESS PRINTER)

WENT TO COLLEGE OF ART & DESIGN, MANCHESTER
STUDIED PHOTOGRAPHIC PRINTING TECHNIQUES -
TO BE A FULLY QUALIFIED FILM MAKE UP ARTIST

APART FROM BEING A PRINTER –
DAVE HAS HAD A VARIETY OF JOBS:
POSTMAN, PROGRESS CHASER,
PRODUCTION CONTROLLER,
ENGINEERING STOREKEEPER/BUYER

AND HAS CURRENTLY TAKEN EARLY RETIREMENT
TO BECOME A CARER & FULL TIME WRITER

DAVE HAS HAD POEMS PUBLISHED IN VARIOUS
MAGAZINES:
WRITE ON, ALLUSIONS, FLY BY NIGHT ETC.
BEEN INVOLVED IN A ROADSHOW '**THE LAST WORD**'
FROM THE COMMONWORD WRITER'S WORKSHOP,
MANCHESTER. IN THE 1980'S

DOING READINGS & SKETCHES AT VARIOUS VENUES,
INCLUDING FOLK CLUBS, LIBRARYS,
CULTURAL & COMMUNITY CENTRES
IN THE GTR MANCHESTER & LANCASHIRE AREAS

ALSO DONE READINGS -
AT NOTTINGHAM UNIVERSITY'S WRITER'S FESTIVAL
REPRESENTING COMMONWORD WRITER'S GROUP
MANCHESTER - FOR WRITER'S CLUBS
THROUGHOUT THE COUNTRY

AND BELLE VUE PEOPLES FESTIVAL, MANCHESTER.
BEEN A MEMBER OF **'THE VALLEY POETS'**
WITH FELLOW POET, GOOD FRIEND
& SOUL MATE ALAN BUTTERWORTH'
(THAT EVOLVED FROM 'THE ORGAN INN',
IN HOLLINGWORTH, HYDE, CHESHIRE)

DAVE HAS ALSO BEEN INVOLVED IN A VARIETY SHOW
AS A DOUBLE ACT WITH FELLOW WRITER
ALAN BUTTERWORTH
(FROM *THE VALLEY POETS*)
CALLED '**PAVEMENT ARTISTES'**
AT THE GUIDE BRIDGE THEATRE,
ASHTON-U-LYNE, GTR. MANCHESTER

APART FROM WRITING POETRY
DAVE'S OTHER INTERESTS
INCLUDE ART (DRAWING & PAINTING), PHOTOGRAPHY
& NIGHT CLUBBING WITH HIS MATES AROUND
MANCHESTER & BURY AREAS

THIS IS DAVE'S THIRD PUBLISHED BOOK OF POETRY
TO THE SUCCESSFUL:
'THE DONKEY STONE & DOLLY BLUE DAYS'
SET IN & AROUND MANCHESTER IN THE LATE 1950'S

& **'OASIS & THE TWISTED WHEEL'**
ABOUT THE CLUB SCENE & STREET LIFE SET
IN MANCHESTER IN THE 'SEXY SIXTIES'

DAVE PRESTBURY - 2008

DAVE'S PUBLISHED BOOK'S
AVAILABLE ONLINE FROM –

AMAZON, W.H.SMITH'S, WATERSTONE'S
BARNES & NOBLE, BORDER'S & LULU.COM